BONERS

BONERS

Seriously Misguided Facts—
According to Schoolkids
by Alexander Abingdon

Illustrated by
Dr. Seuss

Published by
Black Dog & Leventhal Publishers, Inc.
151 W. 19th Street
New York, NY 10011

Distributed by
Workman Publishing Company
225 Varick Street
New York, NY 10014

Designed by Sheila Hart Design, Inc.
Manufactured in Mexico

ISBN-13: 978-1-57912-740-4

Library of Congress Cataloging-in-Publication Data
Abingdon, Alexander.
  Boners : hilarious mistakes, silly misunderstandings, and madcap mix-ups made by schoolkids / by Alexander Abingdon ; illustrated by Dr. Seuss.
     p. cm.
  ISBN 978-1-57912-740-4
  1. American wit and humor. I. Seuss, Dr. II. Title.

  PN6165.A25 2007
  817.5--dc22

                              2007024165

g f e d c b a

Contents

Foreword

The feverish search for information grows apace. People seem to be in a questioning mood, assuaging their thirst for boundless knowledge at the wells of synthetic waters. Learned and semi-learned purveyors of information are enriching—if not the reader—themselves, their families, their booksellers, and their publishers with volume after volume of closely packed and loosely gathered stores of knowledge. *Informatio redivivus.*

It is with the keenest pleasure, therefore, that the editors of this particular book present an "Outline of Misinformation," a "Story of Errors," a "Symposium of Mistakes"—call it what you will. Here are no compilers of fat books on civilization, no tourists into the fallow fields of philosophy, no tracers of the outline of knowledge, only poor innocent harassed blunderers trying to find the right answers to the most uncivilized of mental tortures: the examination.

Out of the mouths of babes comes the material of this book—babes, at least, compared to their forbears among the Story-Tellers. Teachers of history, of literature, of French and German and Latin, of grammar and rhetoric, of the Holy Book and of the spelling book, have racked their memories and remembered such gems of succinct misinformation as "The Acropolis was the she-wolf that nursed Romeo and Juliet" or "Virgil is the mother of Christ." Names have been omitted lest the authors of these treasures, many of whom are now undoubtedly millionaires and statesmen, motion picture actors and mechanical engineers, congressmen and customers' men—perhaps even presidents—should be embarrassed in their lofty positions by evidences of their youthful indiscretions. To the doubting Thomases who read this book and believe it to be wholly or partly manufactured by professional humorists we have only the profoundest contempt, nay, antipathy.

In closing, or rather in opening to the pages that follow, let us tell a parable which might prompt you to temper a too harsh judgment on the mental sins of these young. A youngster arrived home from school with a garish "E" on his examination card. His mother demanded to see the questions which he had flunked so ignominiously. She read the examination paper carefully and turned on her child with a withering look, dismissing him with the comment: "You must be an absolute *marron*."

"Let him who is without sin"—laugh too contemptuously at what follows.

Definitions

Acrimony, sometimes called holy, is another name for marriage.

The Acropolis was the she-wolf that nursed Romeo and Juliet.

An adage is a thing to keep cats in.

An appendix which nobody of any use.

Ali Baba means being
away when the crime was
committed.

Ambiguity means having two wives
living at the same time.

Ambiguity means
telling the truth
when you don't
mean to.

An antidote is a funny story
that you have heard before.

is a portion of a book,
yet has discovered

EXPLAIN THE WORD "ASSET."
When you are making out an account you
subtract the smaller from the larger
amount. That is called assetaining the
difference.

Average means something that hens lay eggs on.

A blizzard is the inside of a fowl.

WHAT IS A BLUE STOCKING?
A stocking that is blue instead of black or brown. One who is a knight of the Garter.

A buttress is a woman who makes butter.

Celibacy was a unit of land in the Mohammedan system.

Celibacy is the crime a priest commits when he marries.

A brazier is the kind of garment the
Italians wore instead of having their houses
heated by furnaces.

A claim letter states that something that was bought a while ago did not last as long as it was told it would and states the claim.

A compliment is when you say something to another which he and we know is not true.

A connoisseur is a person who stands outside a picture palace.

A deacon is the lowest kind of a Christian.

Doldrums are a series of high rocks near the Equator.

The Dauphin was a rare fish that used to
inhabit the Arctic Circle in the middle ages.

Double dealing is when you buy
something wholesale to sell retail.

"Dour" means a sort of help,
as in the hymn, "O God dour
help in ages past."

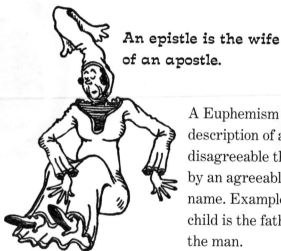

An epistle is the wife
of an apostle.

A Euphemism is a
description of a
disagreeable thing
by an agreeable
name. Example, the
child is the father of
the man.

Faith is that quality
which enables us to
believe what we know
to be untrue.

Genius is
for picki

The Feudal system was that if one
man killed another, the man in the family
of the murdered could kill the murderers.

A fugue is what you get in
a room full of people when
all the windows and doors
are shut.

To germinate is to become a
naturalized German.

A goblet is a male turkey.

A grass widow is
the wife of a
vegetarian.

an infinite capacity
ng brains.

A gherkin is a native who runs
after people with a knife.

Gravity is what you get when
you eat too much and too fast.

**An heir is when
anybody dies you
get what is left.**

WHAT IS AN HERBACEOUS BORDER?
One who boards all the week and
goes home on Saturdays and Sundays.

**An invoice is another
name for the conscience.**

Isinglass is a whitish substance
made from the bladders of surgeons.

Matrimony is a place where souls suffer for a time on account of their sins.

A Mayor is a he horse.

The letters M.D. signify "mentally deficient."

A miracle is something that someone does that cannot be done.

A momentum is what you give a person when they are going away.

A monologue is a conversation
between two people, such as
husband and wife.

Mussolini is a sort of material
used for ladies' stockings.

An oboe is an American tramp.

An optimist is a man who looks
after your eyes; a pessimist
looks after your feet.

Oracles was the greatest orator of his day.
Orator was named after Oracles because
he was the first orator.

The oracle told Laius that if
he had a son, it would kill him.

A protoplasm is a person who is always prophesying.

The Papal Bull was a mad bull kept by the Pope in the Inquisition to trample on Protestants.

The Papal Bull was really a cow that was kept at the Vatican to supply milk for the Pope's children.

Paraffin is the next order of angels above seraphims.

A period is a dot at the end of a sentence.
Period costumes are dresses all covered with dots.

A polygon is a man who has many wives.

A polygon is a dead parrot.

Posters are sheets of paper pasted on blackguards.

A prism is a kind of dried plum, because people say "prunes and prisms."

A prodigal is the son of a priest.

A Senator is half

A Protestant is a woman
who gets her living through
an immortal life.

WHAT ARE RABIES, AND WHAT
WOULD YOU DO FOR THEM?
Rabies are Jewish priests.
I should do nothing for them.

A refugee keeps order at
a football match.

Revolution is a form
of government abroad.

Sans-culottes—That class of people
in France who wore no breeches.

horse and half man.

Scent is the sound made by hounds.

A sinecure is a disease without a cure.

A skeleton is a man with his inside out and his outside off.

S.O.S. is a musical term meaning same only softer.

A Soviet is a cloth used by waiters in hotels.

A vacuum is where the Po

The Sphinx are some people that live in the Phillipine Islands.

A spinster is a bachelor's wife.

The Stoics were the disciples of Zero, and believed in nothing.

The Supreme Cort is our country's cort. It consists of 1 chief justic and 8 sociable justic. What they say goes.

Transparent means something you can see through, for instance a keyhole.

an empty space

pe lives.

Literature
and the Arts

Sir Toby was Olivia's uncle, but otherwise he was no relation to her.

Milton's poetry is full of Biblical illusions.

Tennyson wrote a poem called "Grave's Energy."

Epics describe the brave deeds of men called epicures.

George Eliot left a wife and children to mourn his genii.

An epitaph is a short sarcastic poem.

**Lord Macaulay suffered from gout
and wrote all his poems in iambic feet.**

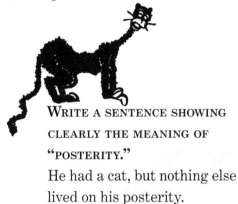

WRITE A SENTENCE SHOWING
CLEARLY THE MEANING OF
"POSTERITY."
He had a cat, but nothing else
lived on his posterity.

**The man looked as if he had
been reduced to posterity.**

Henry pade the fare because of his posterity.

**By his clothes he seemed
a person of great posterity.**

The cat leaped about and then sat
on its posterity.

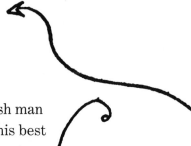

Cassius was a vile selfish man who was always doing his best to make his own ends meet.

Homer was not written by Homer but by another man of that name.

What do you know of King Arthur?
King Arthur collected all the fine brave good-looking young men of his time and called them The Knuts of the Round Table.

Shakespeare lived at Windsor
with his merry wives.

**In conclusion we may say
that Shylock was greedy,
malicious, and indeed,
entirely viscous.**

FROM AN ESSAY ON SHAKESPEARE:
There are some passages in Shakespeare's work,
which are quite pretty, as "Spoil the rod, and bare
the child," and lots of others.

**Shakespeare wrote tragedies,
comedies and errors.**

Tennyson wrote a most
beautiful poem called,
"In Memorandum."

Polonius was a mythical sausage.

WHO SANG, "COME UNTO THESE YELLOW SANDS"?
These sounds were made in the air by Aerial.

Bassanio sang a beautiful
song called, "Tell me, where
is fancy bread?"

FROM AN ESSAY:
I stood on the cliff, the sea was
ruff and the wind roard and not a
sole was to be seen.

King Arthur was a person who was washed
up when a baby, and Merlin said it should be
so and they proved it.

Poetry is a thing you make prose of.

Shakespeare wrote the Merry Widow.

Samuel Johnson was known as
the Doctor of Divinity because
he wrote the first dictionary.

Homer wrote the Oddity.

Most of Shakespeare's plays
were terrible tragedies.

**Pope wrote principally in
heroic cutlets.**

DESCRIBE THE FIGURE OF SPEECH OR
ARTIFICE OF STYLE USED IN THE FOLLOWING:
"THE CHILD IS FATHER TO THE MAN."
Answer: "This was written by
Shakespeare. He often made this
kind of mistake."

OF CHARLES LAMB:
**It was his sister and him who essayed most
of Shakespeare's writings.**

It was Mary Lamb with Charles who between them wrote most of Shakespeare's fairy tales.

Describing Tom Sawyer (Mark Twain): He was a smart looking boy, very fond of fighting, and he was always sharp at this kind of job. His character was always good sometimes.

"Essays of Elia": The attempts of Elijah to get food.

Write a sentence showing clearly the meaning of "asterisk." Last night my father got drunk and made an asterisk out of himself.

"The Lark that soars on dewy wing"
means that the lark was going so high
and flapping his wings so hard that
he broke into prespiration.

The "Complete Angler"
is another name for Euclid
because he wrote all
about angles.

Wells' history is a veritable
millstone on the road to learning.

Milton wrote "Paradise Lost"; then his wife died and he wrote "Paradise Regained."

Keats is a poet who wrote on a greasy urn.

Robert Burns had
one son who was
called Wha Hae.

Poetry is when every line begins
with a capital letter.

Prospero is the clown in
"The Vicar of Wakefield,"
by Dickens.

Virgil was the mother of Christ.

A morality play is a play in which the
characters are goblins, ghosts, virgins
and other supernatural creatures.

Contrary to most of the great poets and authors, Milton's life was pure for he was neither a great drinker or an opium-eater.

Lady Macbeth died of the sleeping sickness.

Keats believed in the immorality of Beauty.

The theme of this poem is that Longfellow shot an arrow into the air, and many years afterward he found it in the heart of a friend.

Name three tragedies by Shakespeare Macbeth, King Lear, and Twelve Nights in a Bar Room.

DEFINITION OF A MEDIEVAL
MYSTERY PLAY:
A play in which the
person guilty of murder
is not discovered until
the final curtain.

Her body was one of a very
strong physique but enclosed in
it was a large tender heart filled
with effection for children.

Horace wrote od

I had an ample teacher last
term. He taught us to do three
things. First how to write briefs
and then to exaggerate them;
second how to extract substances
from novels, and last how to
interrupt poetry.

Chaucer was a great English poet who wrote many poems and verses and sometimes wrote literature.

The Song of Roland was, my country oh! how sweet it seems to me.

Milton wrote Paradise Lost and was a Roman Catholic who graduated at Oxford. He also had a good education.

es and odesseys.

"The Passing of Arthur" is a beautiful poem. It reminds me a lot of "Custer's Last Stand."

Humor was then introduced into the English drama—for example, a wife wringing her husband's neck.

Penelope was the last hardship that Ulysses endured on his journey.

"And doth not Brutus kneel?" means Brutus without his boots on.

When Adam Bede was an old man he entered a convent and became the father of English Literature.

A poetic license is a license you get from the Post Office to keep poets. You get one also if you want to keep a dog. It costs two dollars and you call it a dog license.

bootless knelt

As well as real actors and actresses there are those who we go to see for charity. These are called immature.

The dome of St. Paul's is supported by eight peers, all of which are unfortunately cracked.

Michael Angelo painted the dome of the Sistine Madonna.

Gainsborough painted Mrs. Siddons
as a tragic mouse.

An interval in music
is the distance from
one piano to the next.

Mandolines are high officials in China.

Andrea del Sarto was
not quarrelsome, while
his wife was of the
opposite sex.

Contralto is a low sort of music
that only ladies sing.

Syncopation is
emphasis on a
note that is not in
the piece.

Bible,
Religions,
Myth

In Christianity a man can only have one wife. This is called Monotony.

Laud was a very high-minded man, and thought that every priest should wear vespers and they could expect something if they didn't.

The Grea because of dirty

The message came to Abraham that he should bear a son, and Sarah, who was listening behind the door, laughed.

Job had one trouble after another. He lost all his cattle and all his children and then he had to go and live alone with his wife in the desert.

t Flood was sent of the large numbers people.

WHY WAS JOHN THE BAPTIST BEHEADED?
For dancing too persistently with the daughter of Herodotus.

IN WHAT ORDER DO THE GOSPELS COME?
One after the other.

. . . to love, honour and suckle
my Father and Mother.

If any man smite thee on the right cheek,
smite him on the other also.

The greatest miracle in the Bible is when Joshua told his son to stand still and he obeyed him.

Who was sorry
when the Prodigal
Son returned?
The fatted calf.

Solomon had 300 wives and 700 porcupines.

The saints are classified so that their be one for each kind of human traits, as shipwreck, childbirth, etc.

Abraham was the father of Lot and had ten wives. One was called Hismale, and the other Hagar. He kept one at home and the other he sent into the desert where she became a pillow of salt in the daytime and a pillow of fire by night.

John the Baptist was a centuar which means that he was half a man and half a horse. It says his head was on a charger.

Lazarus used to eat the food out of the rich man's stable.

The Tower of Babel was the place where Solomon kept his wives.

The Mosaic Law was a law compelling people to have their floors laid with coloured stones.

The Pharisies were bad people who used to wash.

Cornelius was the first Gentile virgin.

Jacob was a patriarch
who brought up his twelve
sons to be patriarchs, but
they did not take to it.

Jacob didn't eat much, as a rule,
except when there was a famine
in the land.

Esau was a man who
wrote fables and sold
his copyright for a mess
of potash.

Abraham, after the sacrifice of Isaac,
called the place Rio Janeiro.

A certain man drew his bow at a venture,
but missed the venture and hit Ahab.

The first book in the Bible is Guinessis.

The Bible is against bigamy when it says that no man can serve two masters.

Whenever David played to Saul the latter kept a javelin handy.

Eliza came before the King wrapped in a camel's hair, and said: "Behold me, I am Eliza the Tit-bit."

If David had one a slight tendency

Gomorrah was Sodom's wife. They were both destroyed by brimstone and treacle, and Lot had to flee with them.

When David slew Goliath with a catapult the age of missile warfare commenced. This incident drove the first nail into the coffin of Feudalism.

Little is known of the prophet Elijah, except that he once went for a cruise with a widow.

fault it was
to adultery.

Sarah was Abraham's half-wife, otherwise mid-wife, sometimes called columbine.

Thomas Cranmer was a college student who translated the old Testiment into the new one.

The synagogues were rich Jews who didn't like to work, and believed in Christ.

Before a man could become a monk he had to have his tonsils cut.

Buddha is worshipped

Christianity was introduced into
Britain by the Romans in 55 B.C.

Justinian was the name
given to a group of Christian
friars, whose patron saint
was Saint Justine.

Moses was the crucified son of Christ.

Those who did not accept the
Orthodox faith were hereditary.

chiefly in Budda Pest.

Achilles was the boy whose mother
dipped him in the River Stinx until
he was intollerable.

In the days of Joseph the Egyptians gave refuse to the Israelites.

Ordeals were the bones of saints. They were used to swear an oath upon.

The Wesleyan movement started when the native sultan of the part of India called Wesley tried to get Calcutta. The intention was to stop the commerce of English in that section. The natives were defeated and the Great Mogul killed.

The evils of Mohammedanism were that they believed in thirst and Mohammed was only a lesser profit.

The gods of the Indians are chiefly Mohammed and Buddha and in their spare time they do a lot of carving.

Aladdin was a man who had a ring, and every time he rang a Guinness sprang out of the ground.

Bacchus first taught the Greeks to get drunk.

Medusa was a famous Gorgon and a Frenchman named Zola wrote a book about her.

Plato was the god

Another well-known Greek God
was Appolinaris.

Charon was the man
who fried soles over
the sticks.

Theseus begged Minos to try
and kill the labrynth.

The Gorgons were three sisters
that lived in the islands of the
Hesperides somewhere in the
Indian Ocean. They had long
snakes for hair, tusks for teeth,
and claws for nails, and they
looked like women only more
horrible.

of the Underground.

Geography

Asked to name six animals peculiar to the Arctic regions, a boy replied: "Three bears and three seals."

Grade school pupil who was asked why the Panama Canal would aid in the defense of the country in time of war said: "The locks will keep out the enemy's ships."

Australia sends to England wine made from a bird called the Emu.

Climate lasts all the time, but weather only a few days.

Latitude tells you how hot you are,
and longtitude how cold you are.

**The Menai Straits
are crossed by a
tubercular bridge.**

Sienna is famous for being burnt.

The sun never sets on the British Empire because the British Empire is in the East and the sun sets in the West.

The climate of Bombay is such that its inhabitants have to live elsewhere.

The trade of Spain is small, owing to the insolence of the people.

The Esquimaux are God's frozen people.

The sun sets in the west and hurries round to the east to be in time to rise the next morning.

The people in Iceland are Equinoxes.

NAME THREE ANIMALS
PECULIAR TO THE FRIGID REGION.
The lion, the giraffe and
the elephant would be
peculiar to the frigid region,
but the polar bear, the seal,
and the walrus live there.

People go to Africa to hunt rhinostriches.

Glaciers spread a
murrain over the land.

The highest peak in the alps
is Blanc Mange.

The Arctic regions are neither hot
nor cold, they abound in birds of
beautiful plumage and of no song
such as the elephant and the camel.

Children have hook worm
in the tropical regions.

An axis is an imaginary line
on which the earth is supposed
to take a daily routine.

The equator is a menagerie lion running
round the earth and through Africa.

Imports are ports very far inland.

Nearly at the
bottom of Lake
Michigan is Chicago.

The chief occupation of the
inhabitants of Perth is dying.

The Rhine is boarded by wooden mountains.

The inhabitants of
Moscow are called
Mosquitoes.

**The Pyramids are a range
of mountains between France
and Spain.**

The Eskimoes hardly have any wives at all.

Georgia was settled by thieves and animals taken from the English jail.

A mountain range is used at high altitudes.

An Indian reservation consists of a mile of land for every five square Indians.

The only signs of life in the Tundras are a few stunted corpses.

Among the islands of the West Indies are the Pyjamas, noted for toilet sponges.

Fiume is the name of a
mountain in Japan.

a cooking stove

The whole world, except the
United States, lies in the
temperate zone.

**The people of India are divided
into casts and outcasts.**

Norway's capital is called Christianity.

**Lipton is the
capital of Ceylon.**

The Nile is full of crocodiles and pyramids.

The population of London
is a bit too thick.

China is called China because
the first china was made there.

The North Sea is also
called the German Ocean,
but they don't really
think it is.

Persian cats is the
chief industry of Pers
the word "purr."

England is located on the coast of Great Britain not far from the sea, which makes good fishing.

The Mediterranean and the Red Sea are connected by the sewage canal.

New York stands on the Atlantic sideboard.

The Arctic circle is the circle in the Arctic region where it is day all day long.

ia, hence

New York is behind Greenwich time because America was not discovered until very much later.

Certain areas of Egypt are cultivated by irritation.

The Poles must be 90° from the Equator, therefore they are north and south, because if they were east and west they couldn't be.

Zanzibar is noted for its monkeys. The British Governor lives there.

A water shed is a shed in the middle of the sea where ships shelter during a storm.

Melba—where Napoleon was imprisoned.

The Rialto was the business end of Venus.

Vesuvius is a volcano and if you will climb
up to the top you will see the creator smoking.

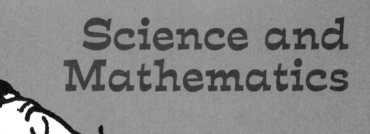

Science and
Mathematics

Science is material. Religion is immaterial.

If there was no nitrogen in
the air we should die of fits
of laughter.

NAME THE THREE RACES OF MAN.
Foot race, horse race and automobile race.

Charles Darwin was
a natulist who wrote
the Organ of the
Spices.

**Huxley was the greatest
antagonist of the
nineteenth century.**

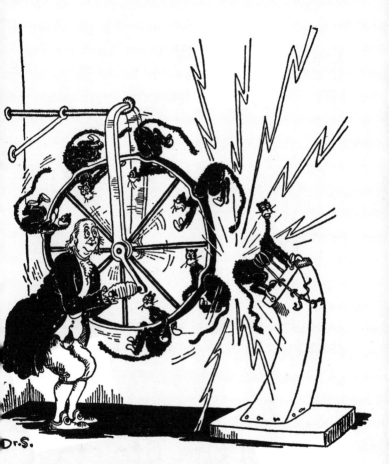

Benjamin Franklin produced electricity by
rubbing cats backward.

A planet is a body of earth
surrounded by sky.

**The solid wastes
are excreted
through the retina.**

The left lung is smaller than
the right one because the soul
is located near there.

**The spinal column is a bunch of bones
down your back to show feeling.**

**A grasshopper p
all the life stages
to adultery.**

The theory of evolution was greatly objected to because it made men think.

The scientific name of the flea is hegira. It was given that name by Mohammet when he went to Mecca.

A grasshopper has three pair of wings—anterior, posterior and bacteria.

The law of gravity was enacted by the British Parliament.

The dog came bounding down the path emitting whelps at every bound.

asses through from infancy

Three kinds of blood vessels are arteries, veins and caterpillars.

The cow gives us milk.
A young cow is called
a calf and gives us jelly.

The cuckoo is a bird that lays other bird's eggs in its own nest and "viva voce."

The pineapple is the

A focus is a thing like a mushroom, but if you eat it you will feel differently from a mushroom, for focusses is poison.

Mushrooms always grow
in damp places and so they
look like umbrellas.

Rhubarb is a kind of celery
gone bloodshot.

The principal parts of the eye are the pupil,
the moat, and the beam.

fruit of the pine tree.

If anyone should faint
in church put her head
between the knees of the
nearest medical man.

A cat is a quadruped, the legs, as usual,
being at the four corners.

To keep milk from turning
sour you should keep it in
the cow.

To pinch a butterfly you pinch its borax.

The zebra is like
the horse only striped,
and is chiefly used to
illustrate the letter Z.

The dodo is a bird that is nearly decent now.

When you stroke a cat by drawing
your hand along its back it cocks
its tail up like a ruler, so as you
can't get no further.

Respiration is composed of two acts, first inspiration and then expectoration.

Man is the only animal who can strike a light.

Quinine is the bark of a tree: canine is the bark of a dog.

The animal which possess the greatest attachment for man is woman.

A sure-footed animal is an animal that when it kicks it does not miss.

A thermometer is an instrument for raising temperance.

Herrings go about the sea in shawls.

Gravity was discovered by Isaac Walton.
It is chiefly noticeable in the autumn,
when the apples are falling off the trees.

**The process of turning steam into water
again is called Conversation.**

To remove air from a flask,
fill the flask with water,
tip the water out, and put
the cork in quick.

**A vacuum is a U-tube with
a flask at one end.**

Chlorine gas is very injurious to the human body,
and the following experiments should, therefore,
only be performed on the teacher.

A litre is a nest

Water is composed of two
gins. Oxygin and Hydrogin.
Oxygin is pure gin,
Hydrogin is gin and water.

The difference between air
and water is that air can be
made wetter, but water cannot.

A magnet is a thing you
find in a bad apple.

Ammonium chloride
is also called silly
maniac.

Our school is ventilated
by hot currants.

# of young puppies.

To fill an apparatus with acidulated water, turn on the taps and acidulate.

Explain the meaning of "erg." When people are playing football and you want them to do their best you erg them on.

The probable cause of earthquakes may be attributed to bad drainage and neglect of sewage.

The tides are a fight between the earth and the moon. All water tends towards the moon, because there is no water in the moon, and nature abhors a vacuum. Gravitation at the earth keeps the water rising all the way to the moon. I forget where the sun joins in this fight.

Three states of water are high water, low water, and break water.

DEFINE THE ELEMENTS.
Mustard, pepper, salt and vinegar.

The earth makes a resolution every twenty-four hours.

The cuckoo does not lay its own eggs.

In some rocks there
are to be found the
fossil footprints of fishes.

When you breathe you
When you do not bre

Polyps swim about the sea when they are
young and when they get old they fasten
themselves on their relations and live like
that for the rest of their lives.

To collect fumes of sulphur, hold a
deacon over a flame in a test tube.

Nitrogen is not found in
Ireland because it is not
found in a free state.

A therm is a germ that creeps
into the gas meter and causes
rapid consumption.

inspire. Typhoid fever may be
prevented by fascination.

athe you expire.

All brutes are imperfect
animals. Man alone is a
perfect beast.

Henry Ford invented perpetual motion.

A MAN HAS *X* MILES TO TRAVEL.
HE GOES *A* MILES BY TRAIN,
B MILES BY BOAT, AND *C* MILES
HE WALKS. THE REST HE CYCLES.
HOW FAR DOES HE CYCLE?
d, *e*, *f*, *g*, *h*, *i*, *j*, *k*, *l*, *m*, *n*, *o*, *p*, *q*,
r, *s*, *t*, *u*, *v*, *w* miles.

Parallel lines never
meet unless you bend
one or both of them.

**A parallel straight line is one that
when produced to meet itself does
not meet.**

DEFINE A CIRCLE.
Take your center and take
your distance and draw a
straight curved line. This is
a circle and all lines drawn to
it are equal.

**A circle is a round line with
no kinks in it, joined up so
as not to show where it began.**

Two straight lines cannot enclose
a space unless they are crooked.

Geometry teaches us to bisex angels.

Algebra was the
wife of Euclid.

WHEN A GRAPH OF "Y EQUALS X²" IS
PLOTTED, WHAT IS THE RESULTANT CURVE?
An eclipse.

Isosceles triangles are used
on maps to join up places
with the same weather.

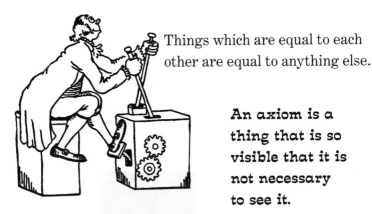

Things which are equal to each
other are equal to anything else.

An axiom is a
thing that is so
visible that it is
not necessary
to see it.

**raical symbols are
when you do not know
you are talking about.**

The logarithm of a given number is the number of times the given number must be squared in order that the given number may be equal to this number.

A circle is a line which meets its other end without ending.

**A polygon
with seven
sides is
called a
hooligan.**

History

Caesar was borned July 12, 100 B.C. he was a great general and a great orator he was well up on his Greek and art. His mother taught him when he was a young boy. He held his first office at the age of thirteen. He fought in many battles. The Ides of March murdered him because they thought he was going to be made king.

Caesar extinguished himself on the battlefields of Gaul.

The Augustan era was a mistake of Augustus.

Attila was the wife of Justinian, and was a great help to him.

Pepsin was king of the Franks.

In the Middle Ages the Pope
had very great sexual powers.

**Medieval commerce was
carried on chiefly in
Venus. She sent her
sailors all over the world.**

DESCRIBE THE HARDSHIPS OF THE CRUSADERS
ON THEIR WAY TO THE HOLY LAND.
Many of them died of salvation.

The wife of Columbus was Columbine.

Joan of Arc was cannonised
by Bernard Shaw.

Martin Luther was nailed to the church door at Wittenburg for selling papal indulgences.

Martin Luther died a horrible death.
He was excommunicated by a bull.

Catherine of Medsi was for breaking away from the Catholic Church but St. Botholomew issued a bill against it and was carried out. This still held the people under the Roman Catholic Church.

Watchword of the
Liberty, Equality

Jean Rousseau: a Frenchman who believed in letting nature take its course. He was against the advancement of civilization. He wrote a book, Society Combat.

The Romans made their roads straight so that the Britons should not hide round the corners.

GIVE KING ALFRED'S VIEWS ON MODERN LIFE HAD HE BEEN ALIVE TODAY.
If Alfred had survived to the present day he would be such an exceedingly old man that his views on any subject would be quite worthless.

French Revolution: and Maternity.

Henry VIII had an abbess on his knee,
which made walking difficult.

William the Conqueror fitted out some
vessels and marched across the land.

**After the great feasts,
William I used to
entertain the barons by
letting off fireworks.**

Next in rank to the overlord
were the beeves.

**King Richard was
captured and put in
prison by the German
Emperor, but the English
people were very fond
of their ruler, so they
boiled him out.**

Magna Charta said that the King was not to order
taxis without the consent of Parliament.

The conquest of Ireland began in 1170 and is still going on.

Edward III been King of mother had

Henry the Fifth was rather a good king, only like many other kings he often went mad.

Henry VIII married Catherine of Aragon. He soon grew tired of her and divorced and beheaded her. He next married Anne Boleyn and also beheaded her. He then married Anne of Cleves and beheaded her—and so on.

Wolsey saved his life by dying on the way from York to London.

would have France if his been a man.

Henry the Eighth was very luxurious. He had six wives—Anne Boleyne was one. When he met her first he flung his handkerchief at her. When he married her the Pope sent him a bull. It drove him into the Protestant Church. Anne Boleyne gave birth to Queen Elizabeth. After her confinement in the Tower, Harry had her beheaded as he wanted to be a widower again.

Philip had made England Roman Catholic, but when Elizabeth came to the throne England was made Christian.

Queen Elizabeth was the "Virgin Queen." As a queen she was a success.

The ancestors of the English people were Queen Elizabeth and Cardinal Woolsey.

The Spanish Armada was where that there was many people without work and it got to be where there were more and more getting without work and was going around begging and the queen tried to stop it but she found that she couldn't and she had them captured and beheaded.

Queen Elizabeth was the Roses, and, fearing that Mary, Queen of Scots, would marry her husband, Sir Walter Raleigh, she beheaded her and in remorse sent Raleigh to discover the United States. When he returned without doing so he was executed by Elizabeth's son, James I, after gaining time to write his long and varied biography in the Tower.

Drake was playing bowls when he was told the invisible armada was in sight.

Queen Elizabeth rode through Coventry with nothing on, and Raleigh offered her his cloak.

James the First claimed the throne through his grandfather because he had no father.

Raleigh died in James I's reign and started smoking.

Cromwell was the executor of Charles I.

The people didn't like King James II and after three years they decomposed him.

William III, on his way to Hampton Court, stumbled over a mole and broke his collar stud—which was fatal to a man of his constituency.

A lot of Englishmen were shut up in the Black Hole of Calcutta with one small widow. Only four got out alive.

They gave Wi funeral. It to the beer.

Queen Victoria was the longest
queen on the throne.

**The Battle of Trafalgar was fought on sea,
therefore it is sometimes called Waterloo.**

The Duck of Wellington won a
big battle and when he finished
he had one arm and one eye and
he looked through the telescope
with his blind eye and said it
was alright and that is how he
won the battle.

**The Prodigal Fathers
sailed for the New World
in 1620.**

lliam IV a lovely
ok six men to carry

**Louis XVI was gelatined during
the French Revolution.**

In 1658 the Pilgrims crossed the ocean and this was known as Pilgrims Progress.

WHERE WAS THE DECLARATION OF INDEPENDENCE SIGNED? At the bottom.

Horace Greeley was the worst defeated candidate ever elected.

EXPLAIN WHAT CLEVELAND MEANT BY "A PUBLIC OFFICE IS A PUBLIC TRUST." A trust is a "conspiracy in restraint of trade." Therefore a public office is a conspiracy to restrain trade.

The President
has a cabinet in
order to keep his
china in it.

Mr. Million is Secretary
of the Treasury.

The chief executive of
Massachusetts is the
electric chair.

Armistice Day is
celebrated each
year to perpetuate
the Great War.

Let us compare the Constitution to a boat with Washington, James Madison and the several others fishing from it with the states as fishes. Some of these little suckers got hooked right off but New York and Virginia, the bass, put up a hard fight in which Patrick Henry took Virginia's part against James Madison. Patrick Henry won but the line was too strong and he along with Virginia came aboard. New York was caught easily and only Rhode Island remained. She would not be caught so they threatened to dynamite the pool, that is, to treat her as a foreign country, so she bit and the thirteen states stood a "New Nation under God."

Language
and Rhetoric

Gender shows whether a man is masculine, feminine, or neuter.

An injection is a shout or scream raised by a person too surprised or frightened to make a sentence with his thoughts. It is not quite a human language. The lower animals say nothing else but injections. Accordingly ill-natured and cross people by their injections come very near to beasts

A metaphor is a thing

A conjunction is a place where tw railway lines meet.

An abstract noun is one
that cannot be heard,
seen, touched, or smelt.

An interjection is a sudden
explosion of mind.

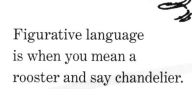

A metaphor is a
suppressed smile.

Figurative language
is when you mean a
rooster and say chandelier.

you shout through.

A proposition is for a country
to have no alcolic drinks in it.

GIVE AN EXAMPLE OF COLLECTIVE NOUN.
Garbage-can.

123

A sentence that does not depend on
any word in the sentence is not
subordinate but inordinate.

Gender is the destruction of sex.

When a word gets out of date
it is termed "dead" and so
gradually a language is built up.

No is the adverb of negotiation.

PUT THE FOLLOWING
WORDS IN A SENTENCE
—BLISS, HAPPINESS.
O bliss, O happiness!

**A passive verb is when the subject is the
sufferer, as "I am loved."**

DEGREES OF COMPARISON OF "BAD."
Bad: very sick: dead.

The masculine of vixen is vicar.

Masculine, man;
feminine, woman;
neuter, corpse.

**Feminines:
Bear, vixen;
Sheep, you.
Masculine of
ladybird: The
masculine of
ladybird sounds
as if it ought to
be gentlemanbird,
but that looks funny.**

The future of "I give"

The feminine of bachelor
is lady in waiting.

**The plural of forget-me-not
is forget-us-not.**

The plural of ox is oxygen.

The opposite of evergreen is nevergreen.

DEFINE THE FIRST PERSON.
Adam.

GIVE THE PASSIVE OF "JOHN SHOT MY DOG."
"My dog shot John."

is "You take."

CORRECT "IT WAS ME WHO BROKE THE WINDOW."
"It wasn't me who broke the window."

WHAT IS THE LAST LETTER
OF THE ENGLISH ALPHABET?
Yours truly.

Habeas Corpus was a phrase used
during the great plague of London, and
means "Bring out your dead."

GALLIA OMNIS EST DIVISA IN PARTES TRES.
All Gaul is quartered into three halves.

DE MORTUIS NIL NISI BONUM.
There's nothing but bones
in the dead.

PASCEBATQUE SUAS
QUISQUE SENATOR OVES.
Every senator
used to live on
his own eggs.

TIMEO DANAOS ET DONA FERENTES.
J'estime les Danois et leur dents de fer.

DIDO VENTO REDITURA SECUNDO.
Dido will come again
with her second wind.

PAX IN BELLO.
Freedom from indigestion.

AVE DOMINE.
Lord, I am a bird.

AGNUS DEI.
A woman composer
famous for her church
music.

LXXX.
Love and kisses.

A.D.
All dates after
Christ or
anteduluvian.

HORS D'OEUVRE.
Out of work.

HORS DE COMBAT.
War horse.

NOTRE VOISIN EST
MORT D'UNE CONGESTION
PULMONAIRE.
Our neighbour died
in a crush on a
Pullman car.

MES SOUVENIRS SONT PEU PRÉCIS.
My recollections are precious few.

TRÈS VOLONTIERS, RÉPONDIT-IL.
Three volunteers responded.

LE PEUPLE ÉMU RÉPONDIT.
The purple emu laid
another egg.

VOICI L'ANGLAIS AVEC SON
SANGFROID HABITUEL
Here comes the
Englishman with his
usual bloody cold.

Miscellaneous

My brother was kicked
because he was wicked
in the seat of his pants.

She was a lion in front and
a dragon in the rear.

When he (Bismarck) died his
brains were examined and he
proved to have been the most
intellectual man of his time.

Our forefathers
are not living as
long as they did.

Seafaring men in the
habit of drinking are
liable to collide with
other vessels.

The serfs were attached to the soil and
when it moved, they moved with it.

Queen Victoria said "we are not much amused" when she went to the pantomime with Prince Concert.

A deacon is a mass of inflammable material placed in a prominent position to warn the people.

Writ of Habeas Corpus means a man is not allowed to commit adultery without permission of the court.

Letters in sloping type are in hysterics.

When a lady and a gentleman are walking on the foot-path the lady should walk inside the gentleman.

Lord Mayors of London are famous city men who are generally benighted.

The Prince of Wales uses a different title when he travels in the Congo.

The shop windows looked very gay; lump sugar, granulated, and castor were arranged in different coloured bowls according to their sex.

All the crew were taken into custardy.

ZEKE
The
Magnificent
Capacity:
335 Litres

The most interesting feature of the zoo was
the largest ape in capacity.

The jockey lost two of his teeth when his horse fell, and had to be destroyed.

The theory of exchange, as I understand it, is not very well understood.

The Pilgrim Fathers were Adam and Eve.

M. Poincaré is known by his saying "Every day and in every way I get it better and better."

WHERE ARE THE KINGS OF ENGLAND CROWNED? On their heads.

Queen Elizabeth was a vurgin queen, and she was never marrid. She was so fond of dresses that she was never seen without one on. She was beautefull and clever with a red hed and freckles.

The wife of a

Henry said, "Beware of the Brides of March."

During the Napoleonic Wars crowned heads were trembling in their shoes.

TEACHER'S DICTATION: "HIS CHOLER ROSE TO SUCH A HEIGHT THAT PASSION WELL NIGH CHOKED HIM."

Pupil's reproduction: "His collar rose to such a height that fashion well nigh choked him."

When we got there our trunk hadn't arrived, so we had to sleep in something else.

duke is a ducky.

False doctrine means giving people the wrong medicine.

Her mother, being immortal, had died.

Socrates died from an overdose of wedlock.

Always choose a good
neighbour, and if you
are lucky enough to get
a bath, have it at once.

**The Press today
is the mouth-organ
of the people.**

Everybody needs a holiday
from one year's end to another.

**There are only two crimes
visited with capital punishment,
murder and suicide.**

Big Bill Thompson is
America's Mustard King.

**A democracy believes in
God and a republic doesn't.**

The King was crowned
in the Crystal Palace with
his sepulchre in his hand.

Lord Bacon was impeached
for deceiving brides.

The first man who went to the
Crusades was Robinson Crusoe.

The Emperor of Japan is called the Mikado, but no
one has seen him since the Middle Ages.

In the United States
people are put to death
by elocution.

The form of government most commonly used in
the cities is keep to the right.

One argument for the abolition of
the jury system is that it costs too
much to buy chairs and to hire
a room for them.

Certainly the pleasures
of youth are great, but they
are nothing to the pleasures
of adultery.

Most bulls are harmless,
but cows stare horribly.

A man who marries
twice commits bigotry

A phlegmatic person is one
who has chronic broncitis.

The different kinds of senses
are commonsense and nonsense.

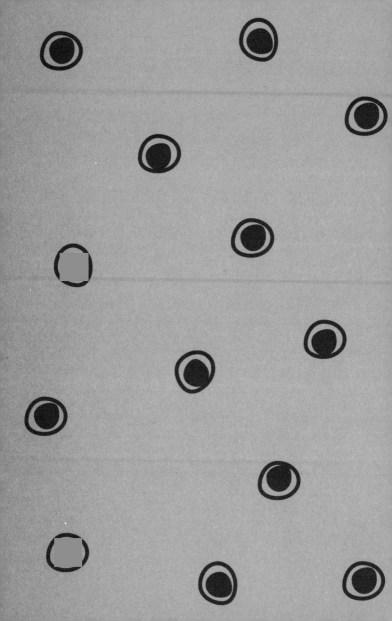